BISON
Distant Thunder

A bull moving through dead lodgepole pines near the Mud Volcano, Yellowstone National Park, Wyoming.

BISON
Distant Thunder

Douglas Gruenau
Preface by Doug Peacock

Winter photographs by Steven Fuller

TAKARAJIMA BOOKS

This book is dedicated to my parents, Ruth Ann and Curt,
for their loving support of my interests as a young naturalist.

Author's note
The title phrase "distant thunder" comes from a George
Catlin quotation found on page 48.
The quotations are taken from many sources and are placed in
the photographic essay to offer the reader other viewpoints.
I only wish I could have taken photographs of the vast bison
herds these people saw.
The authors are identified by brief biographical notes.

AMONG THE BUFFALO SKULLS

From a time on this planet long before our own, herds of totemic bison have thundered through the consciousness of human beings. More than thirty thousand years ago—not long after the appearance of *Homo sapiens sapiens*—images of bison were painted in the dim firelight of Magdalenian torches deep within the recesses of caves near Niaux, France and Altamira on the coast of Spain. On the North American continent, the earliest people followed the twin-crescent tracks of bison south down the ice-free corridors from Alaska. There, on the American Great Plains, the Paleo-Indians left their exquisitely chipped fluted spear-points imbedded in the shoulder bones of prehistoric buffalo, *Bison antiquus figgini*. Twelve thousand years later, the last of the Plains Indian hunters riding their painted buffalo ponies drove iron arrow points into the flank of tatanka—*Bison bison bison,* the American bison, the creature we call buffalo—the greatest animal herds to ever roam the earth.

Some seventy million of these animals were estimated to have ranged over the plains of North America in 1800. A century later, only a few hundred bison existed on the planet. Both the magnitude of this milling, vibrant animal spectacle and the rapidity with which the herds were slaughtered into near extinction are unprecedented throughout human history.

In the spring of 1977, I lived with bison in the wilds of Yellowstone Park. It was late April and three feet of snow lingered under the lodgepoles. I had spent much of the decade here and this was the third spring in a row I had spent a month or more alone in Yellowstone's backcountry waiting for grizzlies to pass through these narrow valleys—the only place in the world American bison have always roamed free.

The place is upper Pelican Valley and the finger meadows reaching north along Astringent and Pelican Creeks. Here the last twenty-three wild American bison on earth eluded Yellowstone Park's efforts to capture them in 1902. Twenty-three wild bison were all they could find! There could have been a few more but not many. About 700 additional buffalo lived in captivity at that time. In less than a hundred years, Americans reduced the quintessential animal of the continent by 99.999 percent. The lightening efficiency of this butchery boggles the mind.

There in Yellowstone, on April 25, 1977, I marked two events on my seasonal calendar: the first, I saw a baby buffalo, the first bison calf of the year, signalling the beginning of spring. The second event was my stumbling across an early historic camp hidden in the timber. I was on a side canyon of Astringent Creek where I had tracked a grizzly up onto the deeper soft snows where I couldn't follow. Taking a shortcut on my way down, I passed a string of hot springs and bushwhacked south into the timber. A short distance into the trees, an axe-hewn stump protruded above the snow. I crossed a patch of open ground, where the snow had been melted by underlying thermal activity, and found fragments of ancient rusted metal. In the clearing were fragments of ancient rusted metal and the neck of a small glass bottle with the seam running up into the lip of the bottle, the kind made by a closed mold, common just before the turn of the century.

The American conservation movement had its beginning right here and the issue was the protection of bison. In 1894, an Army patrol ran across sledge tracks up Pelican Creek and snowshoe prints a mile or so up Astringent. Following the old trail they found a poacher's camp in the timber with six bison scalps hanging from the trees. The detachment followed the creek down Pelican valley where they found a newly erected lodge. Below, in Pelican valley, they saw a man. Shots reverberated over the sagebrush-covered benches.

Edgar Howell was busy skinning a poached bison when the patrol apprehended him. The soldiers hauled Howell and his trophies back to Mammoth Hot Springs to stand trial. On the way they ran into a group of conservationists from *Forest and Stream* magazine. Pictures were taken of Howell and his buffalo scalps. The magazine's editor, George Bird Grinnell, rushed the story into print and took it to Washington where he urged lawmakers to act. Thirteen days after Howell's arrest, H.R. 6442 was introduced by Representative John Lacy of Iowa. On May 7, 1894, the Lacy Yellowstone Protection bill was signed into Law. The Lacy Act was the precursor to the Endangered Species Act and the first federal legislation protecting the bison. For all the other buffalo herds, however, it was twelve years too late.

The national bloodbath known as the Great Buffalo Hunt lingers yet, near the core of our flawed relationship with the American landscape. The decision to exterminate the bison was semi-conscious. The conflict by white settlers with Indians over land control was resolved when official policy linked the two: to exterminate the Indian you only needed to exterminate his commissary, the buffalo. The Army handed out free ammunition to anyone; any dude who could ride the railroad could now shoot buffalo from the train, leaving them to die and rot by the thousands. By 1865, only fifteen million bison were left. By 1880, the killing moved north because the southern and Nebraskan herds were all gone.

Buffalo were killed for their hides, tongues, their bones for fertilizer, for sport, and for the hell of it. Buffalo hunters took the most; their greatest glee was a "stand" where a herd of buffalo milled around a bison shot dead by rifle fire at great distance. You could just keep shooting; a man named Nixon killed one hundred twenty bison in forty minutes this way, stopping only because his rifle overheated. The price per skin dropped to a dollar. Buffalo bones as fertilizer went for twelve bucks a ton. By 1893, all but a couple of herds had vanished. "A cold wind blew across the prairie," observed Sitting Bull.

What this meant to the people whose culture centered around the American bison was the end of life. Plenty-coups, Chief of the Crows, in his autobiography, wrote; "When the buffalo went away the hearts of my people fell to the ground, and they could not lift them up again. After this nothing happened. There was little singing anywhere."

Since that grim spring of 1902, when the total number of wild American bison dipped to two or three dozen, the buffalo has made a recovery. In 1905, President Roosevelt helped found the American Bison Society. Protective measures were implemented and in 1909, the National Bison Range was established in Montana.

Today, in what is called one of the great comeback stories of conservation history, about 120,000 bison live on earth. About 80 percent of these animals are in privately owned herds. Twenty-four Indian tribes have banded together in an Inter-tribal Bison Cooperative, in an effort to expand the numbers and range of the buffalo, to generate income, and to renew their ancient spiritual link with bison. Proposals—such as the Buffalo Commons and the Big Open—to recolonize much of the Northern Plains with buffalo have received serious attention.

Raising bison as food is a large part of this business; buffalo meat is tasty, nutritious, and lower in fat and cholesterol than skinless chicken breast. Already, bison steaks have hit the menus of trendy restaurants in New York and Colorado. A headline in the *New York Times* read: "The Buffalo Returns: This Time as Dinner" and noted: "Animals that people eat do not become extinct."

Not everyone is in favor of bringing back the bison. The cattle industry has generally opposed re-introduction and nowhere have ranching interests been more strident against buffalo than in the Yellowstone ecosystem, especially on the Montana side. The issue is brucellosis, a disease that can cause cows to abort. Whether bison can give it to cattle remains unanswered; there are no documented infections of cattle by wild bison. The tone of the sentiment sounds as much like 1880 (*Indianapolis Star*: "Why [preserve] these ungainly beasts when cattle are beautiful to look at?") as 1990 (Montana state legislator Bob Gilbert: "What bison are, in a nutshell, are big, stupid, ugly cows.").

Nonetheless, the loud and unsubstantiated complaining of the livestock industry has caused the Montana Department of Fish, Wildlife, and Parks and the Park Service to cave in by shooting or removing all buffalo that wander beyond Yellowstone Park's boundaries. One recent winter, 559 of Yellowstone's estimated 2700 bison were killed. The animals that the Park calls the nation's "last free-ranging herd" are systematically shot as they cross the line and thus hardly free to roam. The symbolic expense of our collective inability to reintroduce native, free-ranging bison to their historic range in Montana remains a crushing defeat to those among us who dream of recreating an American Serengeti on the Northern Plains.

What is missing in the bison debate is consideration of the bison as a non-agricultural animal, and the factor of untamed wildness that somehow induced the rapid and reactionary slaughter of nineteenth century herds. This decimation remains an unmended wound in the American psyche and close to the source of our twentieth century national schizophrenia: the old American dream, the hopeful vision of the frontier, replaced with a cast of butchers and murderers. We have yet to come to terms with the cool efficiency with which we dispatched our buffalos, wolves, grizzlies—and the Indians. We need to see the attitude we held towards the land for what it was and ask if it is a sustainable vision of the future.

"Buffalo have power," said an American Indian living in the High Plains during the late nineteenth century, "the spotted cattle of the White Man have no power." This distinction remains the great value of bison today. You don't meditate on a feedlot full of cows any more than you contemplate a herd of angus. But you can bison. The difference is the direction in which they transport our thinking: outward, away from the self and apart from culture as opposed to a tame walk down a domesticated hallway of mirrors.

The bison was carved slowly by nature through millennia to fit into the land they lived in. They were not shoe-horned into the habitat by hybrid geneticists. They live apart from our barnyard selections. A buffalo herd is beyond our agriculture, a tribal society far older and finished than our own.

This crucial distinction of seeing "otherness" either as an extension of our own selective needs, or as independant nations, colors how we have seen and treated all things beyond the boundaries of the familiar—other species of animals, other races and cultures of human beings. It was no mistake; annihilation of the buffalo was linked with eradication of native tribes. The return of the bison gives us a chance at readdressing an ancient historical insult.

We need to eat bison meat once again. But more than we need their flesh, we need to rekindle the ancient contacts we once shared with the animals we hunted; the ethical basis for hunting was a spiritual relationship both to the animal and to the land we both shared.

Just as our intelligence and capacity for language evolved while observing animal herds, we have a simple and abiding need to experience large numbers of living fauna. Perhaps that flush of awe and wonder we get today upon seeing a great flock of birds or giant school of fish, hints at an old human requirement for encountering animal spectacle—for watching multitudes of animals: a herd of bison staining square miles of prairie or a flock of passenger pigeons that would black out the sun for days. It would have taken your breath away. The exotic, privileged pleasure of watching elephants today is merely the tip of an ancient iceberg of animal craving as real as that for air and water.

If the recolonization of large areas of North America with bison can embrace a notion of pre-industrial wildness, attendant with acceptance of the return of native predators—the wolves and grizzly bears—then the creation of a "Buffalo Commons" or "Big Open" is the most hopeful wildlife announcement in decades. And, if bison ranching can resist the agricultural temptation to tinker with breeding and instead lead us back to an intimacy with the earth, the return of the buffalo is indeed good news.

In August of 1993 I bushwhacked across the Mirror Plateau of Yellowstone Park, crossing seventy trailless miles of wild country, utterly alone, backpacking south into the only place in the United States that has always been home to free-roaming American bison. In the wild heart of that trip I crossed a huge thermal area of hot springs, mud pots, and fumaroles depositing yellow crystals of elemental sulfur. Tracks of many bison and a single grizzly threaded through this dangerous and unstable ground—a geologic newborn flake of earth that is the freshest landscape on the continent. In the middle of this belching mile-square inferno lay a central caldera, vented and steaming, the sulphurous soil supporting a few patches of yellow grass and a single stunted lodgepole pine. Under the tree lay a bleached skull of a huge bull buffalo, ancient and perfect, as perfect as any of the hundreds I've run across here in thirty years of walking.

A few cumulus clouds decorated the incomparable blue of the High Rockies. I knelt next to the skull and placed my hand on the corrugated horn casting of the old monarch. His genealogy went back to the time of the glaciers and now he rested here in this brand new land. From my pack I pulled out a feather. I placed the Great Gray owl primary across the bull's white forehead and quietly petitioned the skies:

I wish your children a new beginning.

Doug Peacock

"Oh, give me a home where the buffalo roam" Brewster Higley (1873)

We stood motionless facing each other, the horns on his massive head shining like blackened steel in the early morning sun. In the cold the bison bull's warm breath billowed out of his wet nostrils. After minutes in a motionless stand-off, I stepped slowly backwards a few feet until I stood next to a small sapling tree. Then I waited.

I had come, at dawn, to the Mud Volcanoe area above the west thumb of Yellowstone Lake in Yellowstone Park to photograph the sunrise. The cold morning held the clouds of steam in the air. Scouting out various photographic possibilities, I began to work. While I was finishing, I noticed two bison bulls coming out of the lodgepole pine forest onto the grassy slope about fifty yards away from where I was working. I was on the trail in what seemed to be a clear view of the bulls. They began slowly to graze the grasses on the slope. After completing my work, I waited until they had moved across my exit trail. Then I took a step along the trail to leave, and in that instant one of the bison bulls charged towards me. He covered the distance in a few seconds and stopped at an arm's length in front of me. I felt no fear, held in the bison's gaze, rather the chagrin of helplessness. Finally, after what seemed a long time, the bison bull lowered its head and began to graze. When both bulls had moved off over the top of the slope, I left.

What had been going on in this bull's mind? Why had he charged? Why had he stopped? Did he just want a closer look, and had he sized me up and decided I wasn't a threat? This encounter began my interest in bison which has led me to spend parts of the last ten years trying to portray their lives in photographs. In the process I have learned about their behavior and biology. The details of their massive, dark bodies are not easy to photograph, but observing them has brought me pleasure and joy. I did this photographic work in three national preserves: Yellowstone National Park in Wyoming, Wind Cave National Park in South Dakota, and Fort Niobrara National Wildlife Refuge in Nebraska.

The grassy sandhills seem to swell and roll in the landscape of the Fort Niobrara National Wildlife Refuge. Here, on the mixed grass prairie, there is more sky than earth. At dawn the bison herd drifts like the shadows of clouds over the dew-covered grass. Near my car, I sit down in the path of the grazing herd to watch and listen. I am amazed by the physical mass of these animals as the herd moves across the prairie. Theirs is a casual

A bull during rut strutting along the crest of a hill on a foggy morning, Hayden Valley, Yellowstone National Park.

movement, as if they have come to a consensus on the general direction of travel but not on the route.

It is nearing the end of the bison calving season. As the herd passes by, I listen to the sounds: the bovine, bawling bleats of young calves trying to locate their mothers; the guttural grunts of cows calling their calves; the deep, bellowing roar of a bull amid the cows and calves in anticipation of the rut; the rush of warm air out of wet muzzles; the squeak of pulled grass; the crunch of chewing; and the rustle of hoofed feet.

As the sun arcs higher in the expanse of prairie sky, it heats the earth. The herd slows and stops as casually as it began to move. Some calves approach cows to nurse. Other calves and cows lie down for a doze, sleepily attentive to the sounds in the herd. The cows begin to chew their cud. By mid-morning the prairie pants in the blaze of the sun.

Most bison calves are born in May and within a few hours of birth are able to move with the herd. They are born with cinnamon colored coats that are shed in about two months. Then their color changes to the more familiar dark browns of adults. Within a month of their birth small nubs of horns break through the skin, the beginning of the more formidable adult armor. For most of the year bison herds consist of small bands of cows and calves (from twenty to about sixty animals, often including a few young males) and separate, smaller bands of bulls (from five to about twenty animals). Just after birth the calf comes into contact with its mother, other adult cows, yearlings, and calves its own age, and thus learns its way in the herd. Without the threat of many predators, the calving season is the gentlest time for the young. It is a time for frequent naps, nursing, and play. Early in the morning, an energetic calf, sometimes cavorting with other calves, might run hundreds of yards over the prairie in large loops with its mother as home base.

During the calving season the cow's attention is focused on her calf, and she is always aware of its location. If the calf moves too far away, or is getting into trouble, the cow will call it back to her with a grunt that the calf recognizes as its mother's.

At birth calves weigh about fifty pounds. Those calves born early in the year increase their body weight by more than six times before the snows of late fall, giving them a better chance to survive the winter. In the first month of the calf's life, it feeds exclusively on its mother's milk, which is rich in butterfat. Soon the calf begins to sample plants, and toward the end of the summer, it will graze for brief periods with the rest of the herd. It will depend on milk for some nutrition for seven to nine months. By mid-summer, at the end of the calving season, the rut begins. Bands of cows and calves begin to come together into larger breeding herds.

The image of "vast herds roaming the plains" of North America at the beginning of the nineteenth century is now the stuff of childhood stories. Various estimates have put the number of bison in the early part of the nineteenth century at between thirty million and seventy million. This was probably the most numerous large mammal ever to live on Earth. The North American bison's range extended from central New York to Georgia, south into northern Mexico, west to the Great Basin and north to the Northwest Territories of Canada. The largest population of bison, however, was located in the grasslands, at the heart of the continent. Some early European explorers of North America described the large bison herds they saw in travel journals. Many of these descriptions surprise the modern reader with the accuracy of their observation, though their efforts to place this New World animal into their familiar European context is often amusing. One marvels at the attention to detail in these writings, especially when one considers the many other things these explorers must have had on their minds — such as survival.

In the centuries before European settlement bison and Indian tribes living on the plains coexisted in a natural balance. Many tribes evolved a life adapted to the nomadic bison herds. This buffalo culture constitutes a rich heritage, wherein a pattern of living that followed the rhythms of the herd allowed the tribes to flourish in the harsh environment of the plains. These tribes depended on the bison not only for food but for clothing, shelter, and other wares. They developed great skill at working leather, and as the nomadic life required a portable shelter, the tipi—made from bison hides and wooden poles—was an elegant solution. Perhaps because of a dependence on the bison, the Plains tribes made the animals an important spiritual focus in their religious lives.

Hayden Valley in Yellowstone National Park is perhaps the only place in North America where one can get a hint of what the rich fauna of these grasslands might have been like for native Americans before the beginning of the nineteenth century. Driving north from Yellowstone Lake, one enters the valley at a high point with a magnificent, sweeping vista of the eastern part of the valley. The Yellowstone River, the last undammed major waterway in the West, meanders through the eastern end of the valley in great lazy curves. In the distance is a range of mountains that lead up to Mount Washburn. Three streams—Alum Creek, Otter Creek, and Trout Creek—drain the valley which supports a rich tapestry of wildlife: grizzly bears, black bears, coyotes, moose, elk, mule deer, bald eagles, osprey, sandhill cranes, trumpeter swans, Canada geese, great blue herons, white pelicans, otters, beavers and the largest free roaming herd of bison in the United States.

In Hayden Valley the bison rutting season begins in late July. The adult bulls have been off in their own company most of the year leading peaceful, bachelor lives. During the rut they join larger herds of cows and calves to fight for the right to sire calves. Like a medieval jousting tournament, the rut involves earnest, ritualized combat with formal rules. Often when a bull approaches the herd, he swings his head from side to side and sends out short blasts of air through his nostrils in repeated, challenging snorts. He will often approach a cow in a state of excitement with his tail held high like a banner, a signal of his temper. He then smells her urine to assess the stage of her estrus. Each cow, as she comes into heat, is tended by a bull who follows her through the herd as she grazes. Frequently a cohort of several other bulls of various ages follows the couple around bellowing challenges to the tending bull who responds by out-bellowing his challengers and chasing off the bulls who come too close.

Occasionally another adult bull bellows, paws the ground and perhaps wallows on a bare patch of ground he has cleared. The tending bull will do the same to signal his hostility. As their loud bellowing becomes more frequent, the challenger may walk directly toward the tending male. Then suddenly with a forceful lunge and lowered heads they butt. You can hear the click of their horns as they jerk their heads. These battles are intense but brief. With a toss of his head the winner declares himself, and in the settling dust the loser quickly backs away. Occasionally these battles can lead to serious injuries to one or both of the combatants.

If the cow is not pleased with her suitor during the courtship, she may abandon his attentions and bolt with the cohort of attending males in loping pursuit across the valley. Calves are relegated to the role of confused bystanders and helplessly tag along behind their mothers throughout the courtship. The bellowing and combat that result from tending several cows in succession are exhausting to a dominant bull, and after several weeks, he often withdraws from the competition. He leaves the herd to graze alone quietly in another part of the valley.

The first European Americans to come to the Great Plains were explorers, traders, and trappers. Commercial relationships set up with the eastern tribes of Native Americans created a trading pattern that spread west. European Americans were getting wealthy trading beaver furs, depleting the beaver populations in the East. The search for more beaver pushed commerce west. In the mid-nineteenth century, many European Americans began to move from the East across the plains to settle on the west coast, lured by land and gold. The number of settlers steadily increased, starting in the eastern sections of the grasslands, bringing them into conflict with the Indian tribes that inhabited the plains, eventually displacing or eliminating the Native Americans who lived there. The national policy of settlement also led to the destruction of wildlife. As bison represented the primary

A view with a bison herd across Hayden Valley to the Washburn Range in early autumn. The trunks of the lodgepole pines in the foreground have had their bark ripped and rubbed off by bulls during the rut.

means by which the plains tribes sustained themselves, exterminating bison gave European Americans control over the Native American population. So the forces of commerce, salted with greed, brought about one of the greatest slaughters of wildlife in human history. During the nineteenth century bison were almost driven to extinction.

It is January in Wind Cave National Park. A biting wind blows snow across the hillside through browned grasses. Out of the wind, on the lee side of the hill, the snow comes to rest in drifts. In the mountains this would be a light snow, but here the winds can whip a few inches of snow into a blinding storm. Snow flakes are trapped in the winter wool of a huddled band of bison; some are standing, others resting on the ground. Their body heat melts some of the snowflakes, but the wind quickly blows more onto their coats giving them a white winter glaze. Winter temperatures in the northern plains can reach 40° below zero, with winds of thirty to forty miles per hour, creating the greatest survival test for the bison. By the time the first snow falls, a bison bull's coat has grown about six inches long on the hump and over two inches long on the hind quarters.

As grazing mammals, bison depend on a supply of plant food. In winter this supply can be buried beneath several feet of snow. Along ridges and uplands, snow is blown clear, providing exposed places for grazing the browned grasses of the past summer. Grazing is possible, however, in deep snows because bison can use their massive heads to sweep snow from buried grasses. The breaking of trails in the deep snow demands much energy from bison, and so they tend to move from place to place less frequently in winter.

During winter in Yellowstone, small bands of bison often seek out the warmth of hot springs and geyser basins. This added warmth can help them save vital body food reserves. However, towards the end of winter, the old, the very young, and the infirm can be gaunt from hunger and frequently die in the lean weeks before the spring greening. During the summer after the Yellowstone fires of 1988, I saw the skeletons of at least eight bison from the road that runs through Hayden Valley. The large number of winter deaths in the park was the result of a reduced food supply. The unusually dry conditions of the previous summer and fall had limited plant growth, while much of the existing grass was destroyed by the fires. Dead bison serve as a needed food bonanza for coyotes, ravens, and bears emerging from hibernation. With the melting snows of spring new blades of grass appear, a fresh source of food for the herds, and the bison year begins again.

A view of the Missouri Breaks from the White Cliffs along the Missouri River in central Montana, near one of the camp sites of the Lewis and Clark expedition. This landscape is little changed from the time of the great bison herds.

The shaggy-headed, swaggering bulls, the trim cows, the satyr-horned, curious yearlings and the gangly, spunky calves, all, as they find their way in the life of the herd, speak to me of a wilder time, a time less measured by human profit and productivity. When I first read the journals of Lewis and Clark, who had been commissioned by President Jefferson to lead an expedition to explore the Northwest, I discovered that the prairies had not only been the most important home for bison but also for grizzly bears, elk, and wolves. None of these animals now live wild on the plains. Wildlife has had to pay a tragic price for our taming of the plains. At the present time, some of the drier parts of the Great Plains are losing their human inhabitants. It is exciting to consider that these majestic bison, once driven to the brink of extinction, might be allowed to reclaim a portion of their homeland.

Douglas Gruenau

A bull in early morning sunlight, Fort Niobrara National Wildlife Refuge in the sandhills of Nebraska. The age of a bison bull is indicated by the shape of its horns. As bulls get older, the horns start curving inward. This bison's horns point upward, indicating that he is about six years old.

Calving Season

A bison herd grazing the prairie in a late spring morning, Fort Niobrara National Wildlife Refuge. Bison are the only cattle native to North America.

Their faces are short and narrow between the eyes, the forehead two spans wide. Their eyes bulge on the side, so that when they run they can see anyone who follows them. They are bearded like large goats, and when they run they carry their heads low, their beards touching the ground. From the middle of the body toward the rear they are covered with very fine wooly hair like that of a coarse sheep, and from the belly forward they have thick hair like the mane of a wild lion. They have a hump larger than that of a camel, and their horns, which barely show through the hair, are short and thick. During May they shed their hair on the rear half of the body, and then look exactly like a lion. To remove their hair they lean against small trees found in some of the gorges and rub against them until they shed the wool, as a snake sheds its skin. They have a short tail with a small bunch of hair at the end, and when they run they carry it erect like a scorpion. One peculiar thing is that when they are calves they are reddish like ours, but in time, as they become older, they change color and appearance.

Pedro de Castañeda: a member of the Coronado Expedition to the pueblos of the American southwest and the Great Plains of Kansas in the early 1540s.

A resting bull and standing cow with her young calf, Fort Niobrara National Wildlife Refuge. Most calves are born during a few weeks in May. In the past, large numbers of bison calves born at the same time helped insure that many more young calves survived the threat of predation by wolves and grizzly bears.

In pursuing a large herd of buffaloes at the season when their calves are but a few weeks old, I have often been exceedingly amused with the curious manoeuvres of these shy little things. Amidst the thundering confusion of a throng of several hundreds or several thousands of these animals, there will be many of the calves that lose sight of their dams; and being left behind by the throng, and the swift passing hunters, they endeavour to secrete themselves, when they are exceedingly put to it on a level prairie, where nought can be seen but the short grass of six or eight inches in height, save an occasional bunch of wild sage, a few inches higher, to which the poor affrighted things will run, and dropping on their knees, will push their noses under it, and into the grass, where they will stand for hours, with their eyes shut, imagining themselves securely hid, whilst they are standing up quite straight upon their hind feet and can easily be seen at several miles distance.

George Catlin: a painter and ethnographer of the Plains Indians in the 1830s, from *North American Indians.*

A cow resting with her young calf, Fort Niobrara National Wildlife Refuge. Bison, like other ruminants, spend their days in cycles of grazing and resting to chew their cud.

The Bison is at times brisk and frolicksome, and these huge animals often play and gambol about, kicking their heels in the air with surprising agility.

John James Audubon: naturalist and painter of North American birds and mammals, from *Viviparous Quadrapeds of North America.*

A young calf resting in the prairie grass, Fort Niobrara National Wildlife Refuge. In their first weeks of life, calves need frequent rest. They become more active at about a month of age.

The calving season is May, when the heat of the sun is sufficiently strong for preservation of their young in the open air.

Alexander Ross: a Canadian explorer and fur trader in the early 1800s for the Pacific Fur Company, Northwest Company, and the Hudson Bay Company.

A month-old calf sniffing a young calf. Adolescent calves are very curious, often investigating new-born calves.

A calf running through the dew-soaked grasses near the Yellowstone River in Hayden Valley. Older calves have a great deal of energy and sometimes engage in running games.

Two older calves resting, Fort Niobrara National Wildlife Refuge. After about a month, a bison calf's coat changes color from cinnamon to the dark brown of adult bison.

A young calf standing near its mother, Fort Niobrara National Wildlife Refuge.

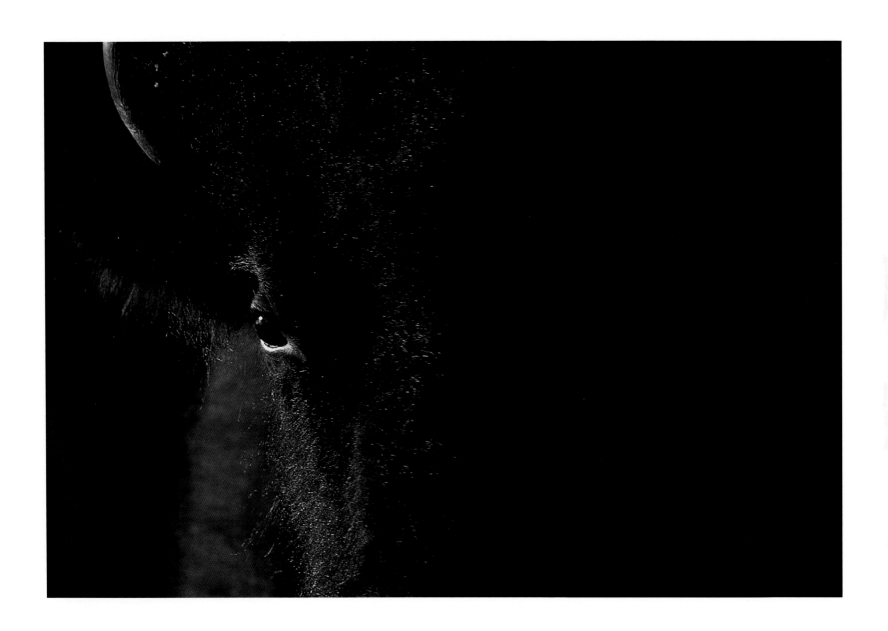

A detail of a cow's head, Hayden Valley, Yellowstone National Park.

August 23, 1691

This Instant y^e Indians going a hunting Kill'd / great store of Buffillo Now y^e manner of their hunting / these Beast on y^e Barren ground is when they see a great / parcel of them together they surround them wth men wch done / they gather themselves into a smaller Compass Keeping / ye Beast still in y^e middle & so shooting y^m till they / break out at some place or other & so gett away.

Henry Kelsey: an explorer of the Canadian prairies for the Hudson Bay Company in order to bring native commerce to the York Factory on Hudson Bay.

A band of bison filing past ponderosa pines in Wind Cave National Park, South Dakota. These bison are walking toward the body of a cow elk that was killed by lightning in a thunderstorm the night before. Bison are often attracted to and excited by the bodies of dead animals, especially other bison. At other times they will chew the mineral-rich bleached bones of bison long dead.

The paths by which they have passed are beaten like our great roads in Europe, and no grass grows there. They cross rivers and streams. Buffalo cows go to islands to prevent wolves from eating their calves; and even when the calves can run, the wolves would not venture to come near because the cows would kill them.

Father Louis Hennepin: a Recollet order French missionary and member of the La Salle Expeditions, 1678–1682, which traveled from the Great Lakes down the Mississippi River to the Gulf of Mexico.

Bison crossing a backwater of the Yellowstone River in Hayden Valley.

A calf on the flank of its mother, Hayden Valley. Because bison are frequently on the move, cows and calves have to keep in close visual or vocal contact to avoid separation.

Two cows with their calves drinking at Trout Creek, Hayden Valley.

Nest of a mourning dove in bison dung and prairie grasses, Fort Niobrara National Wildlife Refuge.

A cow with a young cowbird on its back, Hayden Valley. Birds frequently use a bison's back as a perch. There are not many good viewing perches on the plains.

Two calves nuzzling in the late evening light, Fort Niobrara National Wildlife Refuge. Calves frequently come together with each other in small groups to play.

A cow and her calf at sunrise on a ridge crest, Wind Cave National Park. Calves form bonds with their mothers that can continue for several years.

Rutting Season

Two bulls in a butting match near the Yellowstone River in Hayden Valley. Occasionally the tensions of the rut are so high-strung that a fight can occur when a cow is not the focus of attention.

The *"running season"*, which is in August and September, is the time when they congregate into such masses in some places, as literally to blacken the prairies for miles together. It is no uncommon thing at this season, at these gatherings, to see several thousands in a mass, eddying and wheeling about under a cloud of dust, which is raised by the bulls as they are pawing in the dirt, or engaged in desperate combats, as they constantly are, plunging and butting at each other in the most furious manner. In these scenes, the males are continually following the females, and the whole mass are in constant motion; and all bellowing in deep and hollow sounds, which, mingled altogether, appear, at the distance of a mile or two, like the sound of distant thunder.

George Catlin: a painter and ethnographer of the Plains Indians in the 1830s, from *North American Indians.*

A bull in the herd, Fort Niobrara National Wildlife Refuge. Bison are the largest land animals in North America, with some bulls weighing over two thousand pounds.

An enormous black head is thrust out, the horns just visible amid the mass of tangled mane. Half sliding, half plunging, down comes the buffalo upon the river-bed below. He steps out in full sight upon the sands. Just before him a runnel of water is gliding, and he bends his head to drink. You may hear the water as it gurgles down his capacious throat. He raises his head, and the drops trickle from his wet beard.

Francis Parkman: American historian and traveler in the American West in 1846, from *Oregon Trail.*

A bull, beard wet from grazing in the dew-soaked grass, in the sandhills, Fort Niobrara National Wildlife Refuge. Bison are selective grazers as they feed across the prairie, preferring different grasses at different times during the year.

October 9, 1772

All over the Country where Buffalo resort are many hollow places in the ground, made by the Bulls in the covering [rutting] season.

Matthew Cocking: an explorer of the Canadian prairies for the Hudson Bay Company.

June 16, 1843

The Buffalo, old and young, are fond of rolling on the ground in the manner of horses, and turn quite over; this is done not only to clean themselves, but also to rub off the loose old coat of hair and wool that hangs about their body like so many large, dirty rags.

John James Audubon: a naturalist and painter of North American birds and mammals.

A bull wallowing, Fort Niobrara National Wildlife Refuge. Wallowing can serve several different functions: it can remove an old winter coat, it temporarily removes insects from along the back, and it can act as a substitute activity for aggression during the rut.

August 5, 1843

Daily we see so many that we hardly notice them more than the cattle in our homes. But this cannot last; even now there is a perceptible difference in the size of the herds, and before many years the Buffalo, like the Great Auk, will have disappeared; surely this should not be permitted.

John James Audubon: a naturalist and painter of North American birds and mammals.

A herd at the side of a small stream during the rut, Hayden Valley. In a herd, bulls tend cows when they come into heat. Other bulls challenge the tending bulls, trying to displace them, so the herd is in constant commotion.

A bull sniffing a cow to discover her sexual state, Fort Niobrara National Wildlife Refuge. Substances in a cow's urine indicate to the bull when she is in heat.

An old bull bellowing, Wind Cave National Park. These deep, guttural bellows resemble the sound of a lion's roar and can be heard over a mile away. The constant bellowing during the rut requires great physical strength from the mature bulls and plays an important role in determining which bulls are most fit.

We had gone scarcely a mile when an imposing spectacle presented itself. From the river bank on the right, away over the swelling prairie on the left, and in front as far as we could see, extended one vast host of buffalo. The outskirts of the herd were within a quarter of a mile. In many parts they were crowded so densely together that in the distance their rounded backs presented a surface of uniform blackness; but elsewhere they were more scattered, and from amid the multitude rose little columns of dust where the buffalo were rolling on the ground. Here and there. . .battle was going forward among the bulls. We could distinctly see them rushing against each other, and hear the clattering of their horns and their hoarse bellowing.

Francis Parkman: American historian and traveler in the American West, from *Oregon Trail*.

Two bulls in combat in Hayden Valley. The force of the blow is so powerful that the dirt along one bull's flank is shaken lose.

June 23, 1820

he rutting season occurs towards the latter part of July, and continues until the beginning of September, after which month the cows separate from the bulls, in distinct herds, and bring forth their calves in April. The calves seldom separate themselves from the mother under the age of one year; and cows are often seen accompanied by the calves of three seasons.

Edwin James: a botanist and geologist on the Long Expedition which explored the Great Plains to the Rocky Mountains.

Two bulls pursuing a cow with her calf at dusk, Wind Cave National Park. Cows play an important role in mate selection. A cow can leave if she isn't satisfied with her choices.

A herd in the early morning fog, Hayden Valley, Yellowstone National Park.

A bull resting next to a small stream, Hayden Valley.

Two young bulls drinking at a small stream, Hayden Valley. Bison must move to water several times a day to get the many gallons of water they need.

A bull in the sandhills, Fort Niobrara National Wildlife Refuge.

A young bull resting after taking a drink in a shallow backwater of the Yellowstone River, Hayden Valley.

The whole world is coming,
A nation is coming, a nation is coming,
The Eagle has brought the message to the tribe.
The father says so, the father says so.

Over the whole earth they are coming.
The buffalo are coming, the buffalo are coming,
The Crow has brought the message to the tribe,
The father says so, the father says so.

Traditional **Lakota** (Sioux) tribal song

A small band of bison crossing the Yellowstone River at dusk, Hayden Valley. Bison are competent swimmers. Even young calves can make a river crossing safely.

June 2, 1810

Pemican, a wholesome, well tasted nutritious food, upon which all persons engaged in the Furr Trade mostly depend for their subsistence during the open season; it is made of the lean and fleshy parts of the Bison dried, smoked and pounded fine; in this state it is called Beat Meat: the fat of the Bison is of two qualities, called hard and soft; the former is from the inside of the animal, which when melted is called hard fat (properly grease), the latter is made from the large flakes of fat that lie on each side of the back bone, covering the ribs, and which is readily separated, and when carefully melted resembles Butter in softness and sweetness. Pimmecan is made up in bags of ninety pounds weight, made of the parchment hide of the Bison with the hair on; the proportion of the Pemmecan when best made for keeping is twenty pounds of soft and the same of hard fat, slowly melted together, and at a low warmth poured on fifty pounds of Beat Meat, well mixed together, and closely packed in a bag of about thirty inches in length, by near twenty inches in breadth, and about four in thickness which makes them flat, the best shape for stowage and carriage. On the great Plains there is a shrub bearing a very sweet berry of a dark color, much sought after, great quantities are dried by the Natives; in this state, these berries are as sweet as the best currants, and as much as possible mixed to make Pemmecan.

David Thompson: a Hudson Bay Company explorer in western Canada.

A cow with cowbirds at sunset, Fort Niobrara National Wildlife Refuge. Cowbirds are nest parasites, laying their eggs in the nests of other songbirds. This is an adaptation which allows cowbirds to follow bison herds, feeding on insects scared up as the bison's hooves shuffle through the grass.

July 4, 1843

As we were riding slowly along this afternoon, clouds of dust in the ravines among the hills to the right suddenly attracted our attention, and in a few minutes column after column of buffalo came galloping down, making directly to the river. By the time the leading herds had reached the water, the prairie was darkened with the dense masses. Immediately before us, when the bands first came down into the valley, stretched an unbroken line, the head of which was lost among the river hills on the opposite side, and still they poured down from the ridge on our right. From hill to hill the prairie bottom was certainly no less than two miles wide, and allowing the animals to be ten feet apart, and only ten in a line, there were already 11,000 in view. Some idea may thus be formed of their number when they had occupied the whole plain. In a short time they surrounded us on every side, extending for several miles in the rear, and forward, as far as the eye could reach, leaving around us as we advanced, an open space of only two or three hundred yards.

John Charles Fremont: a Lieutenant in the US Army Corps of Topographical Engineers who helped conduct the "Great Reconnaissance" of the American West.

A bison band on a trail through the frosted grasses of late summer, Hayden Valley. Bison often reuse the same trails to travel from one place to another.

Two bulls, in the herd, taking the measure of each other during the rut,
Hayden Valley.

August 5, 1820

The wind ceased during the night, and the lowing of the thousands of bisons that surrounded us in every direction, reached us in one continual roar. This harsh and guttural noise, intermediate between the bellowing of the domestic bull and the grunting of the hog, was varied by the shrill bark and scream of the jackals [coyotes], and the howling of the white wolves.

Thomas Say: a zoologist on the Long Expedition which explored the Great Plains to the Rocky Mountains.

Cows and calf at sunset, Fort Niobrara National Wildlife Refuge.

In my youthful days, I have seen large herds of buffalo on these prairies, and elk were found in every grove, but they are here no more, having gone towards the setting sun. For hundreds of miles no white man lived, but now trading posts and settlers are found here and there throughout the country, and in a few years the smoke from their cabins will be seen to ascend from every grove, and the prairie covered with the cornfields...

Shabonee: a peace chief and spokesman for the Potawatomi of the eastern prairies, 1827.

A bull standing near the Yellowstone River, Hayden Valley. The hump on the back is created by long bone spikes on the vertebrae of the backbone.

Cattle [Bison] come as far as here. I have seen them three times, and eaten of their meat. I think they are about the size of those in Spain. They have small horns like the cows of Morocco, and the hair very long and flocky like that of the merino. Some are light brown and others black. To my judgement the flesh is finer and fatter than the beef of this country [Spain]. The Indians make blankets of those not full grown, and of the larger they make shoes and bucklers.

Alvar Nuñez Cabeza de Vaca: a Spanish nobleman and conquistador, who was the first European to cross the North American continent in the area of south Texas and northern Mexico in the 1530s.

A bull resting next to a thermal pool, Yellowstone National Park.

The Miamis hunt them at the end of autumn in the following manner:

When they see a herd, they gather in great numbers, and set fire to the grass every where around these animals, except some passage which they leave on purpose, and where they take post with their bows and arrows. The buffalo, seeking to escape the fire, are thus compelled to pass near these Indians, who sometimes kill as many as a hundred and twenty in a day.

Father Louis Hennepin: a Recollet order French missionary and member of the La Salle Expeditions, 1678–1682, which traveled from the Great Lakes down the Mississippi River to the Gulf of Mexico.

A young bull backed by a wall of steam from a geyser basin, Yellowstone National Park.

Winter Season

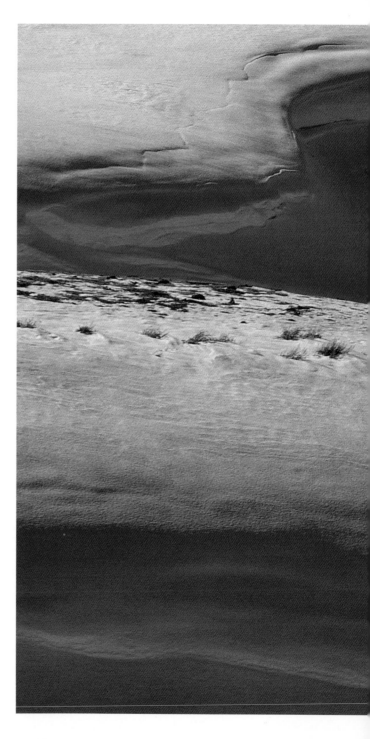

Two bison standing on a wind-cleared knoll below a snow cornice in Hadyen Valley.

Steven Fuller

May 29, 1805

Today we passed on the Stard. side the remains of a vast many mangled carcases of Buffalow which had been driven over a precipice of 120 feet by the Indians and perished; the water appeared to have washed away a part of this immence pile of slaughter and still their remained the fragments of at least a hundred carcases they created a most horrid stench. in this manner the Indians of the Missouri distroy vast herds of buffaloe at a stroke; for this purpose one of the most active and fleet young men is scelected and [being] disguised in a robe of buffaloe skin, having also the skin of the buffaloe's head with the years and horns fastened on his head in form of a cap, thus caparisoned he places himself at a convenient distance between a herd of buffaloe and a precipice proper for the purpose, which happens in many places on this river for miles together; the other indians now surround the herd on the back and flanks and at a signal agreed on all shew themselves at the same time moving forward towards the buffaloe; the disguised indian or decoy has taken care to place himself sufficiently nigh the buffaloe to be noticed by them when they take to flight and runing before them they follow him in full speede to the precepice, the cattle behind driving those in front over and seeing them go do not look or hesitate about following untill the whole are precipitated down the precepice forming one common mass of dead an mangled carcases; the [Indian] decoy in the mean time has taken care to secure himself in some cranney or crivice of the clift which he had previously prepared for that purpose.

Meriwether Lewis: a leader of the Lewis and Clark Expedition, which explored the land along the Missouri River and the Pacific Northwest.

Bison feeding on browned grasses beneath a light dusting of snow near Violet Creek, Hayden Valley.

Steven Fuller

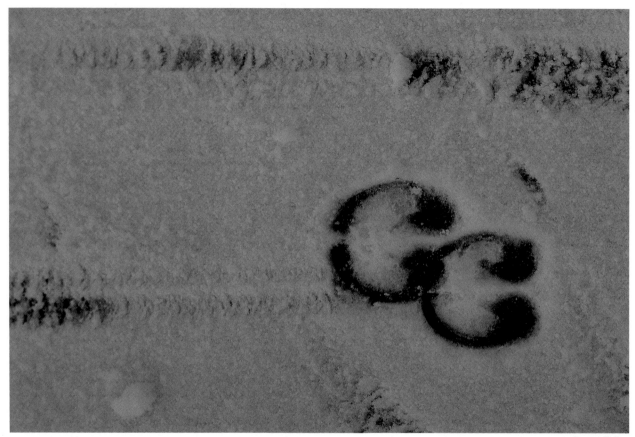

Steven Fuller

Bison tracks in light snow in the Mud Volcano area, Yellowstone National Park.

Bull drinking on a frosty morning in November at the Yellowstone River, Hayden Valley.

Steven Fuller

These buffalo subsist in all seasons of the year. When they are surprised by winter. . . and the ground is all covered with snow, they have the skill to break through the snow and shove it aside, to crop the grass hidden beneath.

Father Louis Hennepin: a Recollet order French missionary and member of the La Salle Expeditions, 1678–1682, which traveled from the Great Lakes down the Mississippi River to the Gulf of Mexico.

Bull feeding on winter grasses after clearing a space in the snow with his muzzle, Hayden Valley.

Steven Fuller

During severe winters the buffaloes become very poor, and when the snow has covered the ground for several months to the depth of two or three feet, they are wretched objects to behold.

John James Audubon: naturalist and painter of North American birds and mammals, from *Viviparous Quadrapeds of North America.*

Dying bull near the Yellowstone River, Hayden Valley.

Steven Fuller

Coyote feeding on a bison carcass in Pelican Valley, Yellowstone National Park.

A frosty bison carcass stripped to little more than hair, hide and bones near Buffalo Ford on the Yellowstone River, Yellowstone National Park.

Steven Fuller

One day a herd came in our direction like a great black cloud, a threatening moving mountain, advancing towards us very swiftly and with wild snorts, noses almost to the ground and tails flying in midair. I haven't any idea how many there were but they seemed to be innumerable and made a deafening terrible noise. As is their habit, when stampeding, they did not turn out of their course for anything. Some of our wagons were within their line of advance and in consequence one was completely demolished and two were overturned.

Catherine Haun: an Iowa bride heading in a wagon train to the California gold rush in 1849.

A young adult bison in a thermal pool in the Mud Volcano area, Yellowstone National Park. During the winter bison will often stand in shallow thermal pools for warmth.

Steven Fuller

The buffalo saw that their day was over. They could protect their people no longer. Sadly, the last remnant of the great herd gathered in council, and decided what they would do.

The Kiowas were camped on the north side of Mount Scott, those of them who were still free to camp. One young woman got up very early in the morning. The dawn mist was still rising from the Medicine Creek, and as she looked across the water, peering through the haze, she saw the last buffalo herd appear like a spirit dream.

Straight to Mount Scott the leader of the herd walked. Behind him came the cows and their calves, and the few young males who had survived. As the woman watched, the face of the mountain opened.

Inside Mount Scott the world was green and fresh, as it had been when she was a small girl. The rivers ran clear, not red. The wild plums were in blossom, chasing the redbuds up the inside slopes. Into this world of beauty the buffalo walked, never to be seen again.

Part of the **Kiowa** tale "The Buffalo Go" told by Old Lady Horse (Spear Woman).

A lone bull at sunset, Fort Niobrara National Wildlife Refuge. After several weeks in the herd, mature bulls will often go off by themselves during rutting season to rest from the rigors of the mating ritual.

I rise, I rise,
I whose tread makes the earth rumble.

I rise, I rise,
I, in whose thighs there is strength.

I rise, I rise,
I, who whips his back with his tail when in rage.

I rise, I rise,
I, in whose humped shoulder there is power.

I rise, I rise,
I, who shakes his mane when angered.

I rise, I rise,
I, whose horns are sharp and curved.

Traditional **Osage** tribal song

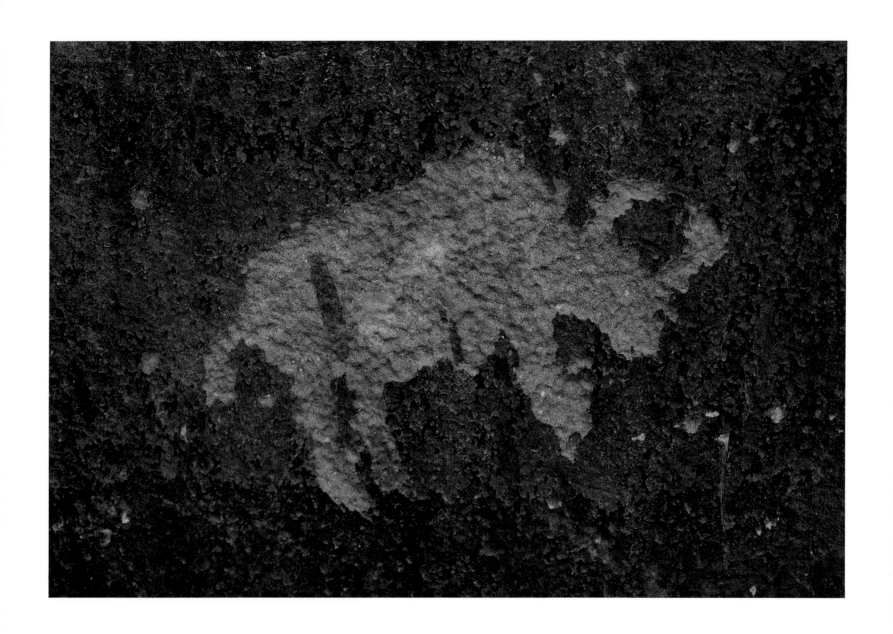

Range of the bison

circa 1500
circa 1870

Size of present herds
(Public, private, tribal)

· 1-500 bison
● More than 500 bison

Private herds included are owned
by members of the Canadian and
American Bison Associations.

0   400
MILES
NGS CARTOGRAPHIC DIVISION

98°W

98°W

ALASKA (U.S.A.)
YUKON TERRITORY
NORTHWEST TERRITORIES
BRITISH COLUMBIA
ALBERTA
SASK.
MANITOBA
NEWFOUNDLAND
QUEBEC
CANADA
UNITED STATES
WASH.
OREG.
IDAHO
MONT.
N. DAK.
MINN.
ONTARIO
MICHIGAN
N.B.
P.E.I.
N.S.
ME.
VT
N.H.
MASS.
N.Y.
R.I.
CONN.
YELLOWSTONE NATIONAL PARK
CUSTER STATE PARK
WIND CAVE N.P.
WYO.
S. DAK.
WIS.
TRANSCONTINENTAL RAILROAD
NEV.
UTAH
NEBR.
IOWA
Omaha
ILL.
IND.
OHIO
PA.
N.J.
MD.
DEL.
Washington, D.C.
San Francisco
CALIF.
COLO.
KANS.
MO.
KY.
W.VA.
VA.
N O R T H
A M E R I C A
G R E A T   P L A I N S
R O C K Y   M O U N T A I N S
ARIZ.
N. MEX.
OKLA.
ARK.
TENN.
N.C.
S.C.
U.S.
MEXICO
TEXAS
LA.
MISS.
ALA.
GA.
FLA.

Pacific
Ocean

Atlantic
Ocean

Gulf of
Mexico

Cartographic Division © National Geographic Society

NORTH AMERICAN BISON FACTS

Classification: Another common name for Bison is Buffalo. Bison are split-hoofed ruminants (cud chewers) and belong to the cow family.

Scientific Name: Bison

Description: The mature male has a large shoulder hump, a set of permanent cattle-like curved horns and coarse hair on the head, neck, shoulders, and front legs.

Body Size: Males can be up to 6 feet tall at their hump and up to 9 feet in length. The tips of horns can spread 30 inches apart. An 8-year-old bull usually weighs about 1650 pounds, but it is not uncommon for them to exceed 2000 pounds. This makes them the largest North American animal. Mature females weigh from 850 to 1100 pounds and are 4½ to 5½ feet at the hump. Yearling Bison weigh about 400 pounds and have 5-inch spiked horns. Calves at birth weigh about 50 pounds.

General Behavior: Bison live in herds consisting of smaller bands. The males often live in bachelor bands for much of the year and come into the mixed herds made up mostly of cows and calves during the rut (mating season), in late July and August. Females tend to lead the movement of these herds. The calves follow their mothers and may nurse for seven to nine months. The Bison like to wallow, that is, dust themselves, by rolling in dirt that they have cleared of grass with their hooves and horns. This is usually done to rid themselves of insect pests. Bulls also wallow to indicate excitement during the rut. Bison are herbivores, feeding on grasses and occasionally other vegetation.

Other Facts: The gestation period is 9½ months. Most calves are born in May. Bison can live to about 20 years of age in the wild. The top running speed of Bison for short distances is about 35 miles per hour.

Population Numbers: Presently there are about 70,000 Bison living in national and state/provincial parks, wildlife refuges and ranches in North America. However, at the beginning of the nineteenth century, various estimates suggest that Bison numbered more than 30,000,000.

Some Places to See Bison: Yellowstone National Park, in the northwestern corner of Wyoming, has the largest wild herd of Bison in the United States, with total numbers in the park exceeding 2000. Solitary bulls can be seen at many places in the park. In summer the best place to see bands of Bison is from the road in Hayden Valley. **The National Bison Range**, located in western Montana near Missoula, manages a Bison herd that numbers over 300 animals and can be seen from a one-way dirt road that winds around the hilly range. **Custer State Park**, in the Black Hills of South Dakota, has a managed herd of about 1000 which can be seen from the roads that run through this 73,000-acre park. **Wood Buffalo National Park** is a large park (about four times the size of Yellowstone National Park) spreading from the northeast corner of the Province of Alberta into the Northwest Territories of Canada. Its remoteness makes the Bison less accessible than in other parks, but it contains the largest population of free-roaming Bison in the world, about 4000. Other places to see Bison include **Wichita Mountains National Wildlife Refuge**, Oklahoma; **Fort Niobrara National Wildlife Refuge**, Nebraska; **Wind Cave National Park**, South Dakota; **Badlands National Park**, South Dakota; **Theodore Roosevelt National Park**, North Dakota; and **Grand Teton National Park**, Wyoming.

Acknowledgements

I want to thank several people who helped me make this book: the staff at Fort Niobrara National Wildlife Refuge in Nebraska, who gave me access to the refuge; Edmund White and the late George Daly, who both read drafts of the manuscript and gave me important suggestions; Richard Whelan, whose encouragement and belief in the project along with his wise advice on the manuscript, photographs and captions helped shape the book; Tomiyasu Shiraiwa, whose interest, skill and dedication in designing the book has made it so beautiful; Akihiko Miyanaga and Kiyotaka Yaguchi, who as publisher and assistant publisher with Takarajima Books transformed idea to book. Finally, I want to thank Brad Richardson who accompanied me on many of the photographic trips and who read the manuscript in all the stages of its development giving me crucial editorial advice.

Bison: Distant Thunder
Copyright © 1995 by Takarajima Books, Inc.
Photographs and Texts copyright © 1995 by Douglas Gruenau
Photographs "Winter Season" copyright © 1995 by Steven Fuller
Preface copyright © 1995 by Doug Peacock

Selected excerpt from *American Indian Mythology* by Alice Marriot and Carol K. Rachlin. Copyright © 1968 by Alice Marriot and Carol K. Rachlin. Reprinted by permission of HarperCollins Publishers, Inc.

Takarajima Books
200 Varick Street, New York, NY 10014
Tel: (212) 675-1944; Fax: (212) 255-5731

Book and Jacket Design: Tomiyasu Shiraiwa

The staff at Takarajima Books for *Bison: Distant Thunder* is:
Akihiko Miyanaga, Publisher
Kiyotaka Yaguchi, Assistant Publisher

ISBN: 1-883489-07-5

Library of Congress Card Number: 94-060217

Printed and bound by C & C Offset Printing Co., Ltd., Hong Kong